Dog Treats

Dog Treats

An Assortment of Mutts, Mongrels, Puppies and Pooches

CHRISTOPHER MATTHEW

Illustrations by Tony Ross

Little, Brown

LITTLE, BROWN

First published in Great Britain in 2014 by Little, Brown

A CIP catalogue record for this book
is available from the British Library.

ISBN 978-1-4087-0566-7

Typeset in Minion by M Rules
Printed and bound in Great Britain by
Clays Ltd, St Ives plc

MIX
Paper from
responsible sources
FSC® C104740

Little, Brown
An imprint of
Little, Brown Book Group
100 Victoria Embankment
London EC4Y 0DY

An Hachette UK Company
www.hachette.co.uk

www.littlebrown.co.uk

To our Kerry Blue terriers, past and present –
Kerrels, Milly, Hal, and now Tippy

Contents

Introduction

'I can't think how anyone can live without a dog' is a phrase that is often to be heard on the lips of my dear wife and the mother of my children – a woman whom I would not be able to describe in such terms had I not been a dog-lover myself.

Kerry Blue terriers are our dog of choice and have been for the past thirty-five years. There was one in residence when I first met my wife in the early seventies. She was called Kerrels (the terrier, that is) and, as one brought up with dachshunds, it took me a while to establish a working relationship with an animal that was a good deal larger, hairier and more boisterous than anything I had been used to.

Kerrels's attitude to me was no less cool and for some time her gaze was (to quote P. G. Wodehouse on the subject of a similarly hairy dog in a Blandings novel) 'cold, wary and suspicious, like that of a stockbroker who thinks someone is going to play the confidence trick on him'.

Happily we developed a warm relationship and Kerrels became a central figure in both our lives.

Her successors have proved to be similarly whole-hearted

members of the Matthew family: Milly, who used to come sailing with me and was the most easy-going crew I ever had; Hal, who had an over-developed sense of responsibility which he was never quite up to fulfilling; and, for the last eight years, Tippy, who in another life would have made a very good chairman of the local neighbourhood watch.

A friend once remarked of Kerrels that he thought she was really a human being wearing a dog outfit. I am not one to anthropomorphise animals, but I have counted all our dogs as close and much loved friends.

It is for this reason that many of the poems in this book are written from the dogs' point of view. I may have invested some of my subjects with thoughts and motives of which no animal could possibly be capable, but when you have experienced the very real feelings that a dog has for its owner, the sheer strength of will that many possess, and the huge range of human characteristics that all breeds display, you can't help thinking that there is a lot more going on in those furry heads than scientists would have us believe.

Emily Dickinson went further. 'Dogs are better than humans,' she wrote, 'because they know but do not tell.'

When my wife let slip to her many dog-walking friends that I was planning to write a book of poems about dogs, their owners and the eccentricities of both, several of them had stories to contribute – some funny, some sad, some bizarre, all well worth adapting into a few lines of rhyming verse. They have my grateful thanks, even if I cannot guarantee that they will necessarily recognise themselves, or their dogs.

Many famous owners have had heart-warming things to say

about their dogs, but none has expressed more lyrically the pleasure that they bring to our lives than Milan Kundera: 'Dogs are our link to paradise. To sit with a dog on a hillside on a glorious afternoon is to be back in Eden where doing nothing was not boring – it was peace.'

Groucho Marx put it another way: 'Outside of a dog, a book is man's best friend. Inside of a dog it's too dark to read.'

Dog Treats

Puppy Love

When Dad comes home at half past six,
I'm on him like a shot;
With leaps and bounds and slurps and licks
I give him all I've got.

I couldn't love a human more;
That's why I treat him rotten;
Then carry on as heretofore,
Attending to my bottom.

A Dog's Dinner

Our terrier Ted's a gastronome –
A dog who's very much at home
Where gourmet food is de rigueur,
And butter's often known as *beurre*,
And lobster is the scrap of choice,
And travel is by green Rolls-Royce.
Young Ted's a superstar chez nous –
A canine classic through and through:
A sort of doggy A. A. Gill,
Without the bite. His biggest thrill
Is lying very, very low
While waiting for our guests to go,
And, just as soon as he is able,
Climbing on the dining table
And scoffing anything that's left
With speed and skill one might call deft.
And not just food, but booze as well,
From Beaujolais and Muscatel
To coffee (black) and herbal tea,
While smidgens of the ripest Brie
And little blobs of chocolate mousse
(Mixed here and there with raspberry juice)
Are lapped up with a long pink tongue –
In terrier's terms, the perfect bung.

One night, amid the farewell schmooze,
Ted overdid it with the booze.
He polished off a glass of port,
And, rather as an afterthought,
A long-abandoned single malt:
It really wasn't *all* his fault.

The full effects were all too clear
As Ted turned obviously queer,
Beginning with a carefree pee
Against the custom-built settee,
While looking maddeningly smug,
Then puking on a Persian rug,
And crashing through the kitchen door,
And falling senseless on the floor.

Of course, we kicked up quite a stink.
From then on, Ted was off the drink –
And off the table, as it goes,
Along with his all-questing nose.

On dinner party nights, off-stage,
Incarcerated in his cage,
He now eats simple, homespun grub –
The sort you might get in the pub:
A fillet steak or chopped-up gammon,
Some lightly poached organic salmon,
A bowl of Highland Spring (not fizzy),
A toy to chew and keep him busy.

A dog that wears a human face
Is happier when he knows his place.

A Rose by Any Other Name

Now you can't call a puppy dog Eric,
Or Alan, or Graham, or Bruce,
Or Robin, or Norman, or Derek,
And to do so is plainly obtuse.

But some owners are not to be daunted;
For them any name would sound sweet.
If their poodle was Balzac, they'd flaunt it;
There's no limit to some folks' conceit.

It's a brave man who calls his dog Jesus,
And a braver one still who owns God;
And we know that there's some wag who'd tease us,
If we dared to shout 'Sit, Ichabod!'

You may smirk when an owner yells 'Rover!'
And 'Buster!' and 'Rex!' risk a laugh,
But the words 'Put it down, Casanova!'
Could disable a small seismograph.

Yet my cousins were really offended
The weekend they came down to stay,
When we said we'd not quite comprehended
Why they'd called their Great Dane Cher Bébé.

As names go, it's plain idiotic,
As the poor mutt knows better than they.
He is plain-as-a-pikestaff psychotic,
And in all probability gay.

When the fool did a runner at midnight,
And they shouted his name for an hour,
He ignored them, as any bright kid might:
We had no other choice but to cower.

Now we may have to think relocation;
We are getting some very odd looks.
The fact is that sheer affectation
Is a habit that nobody brooks.

Hooray for Hollywood?

My owner is an actress,
A model and DJ,
A long-time benefactress
Of causes in LA.

An author and designer,
A business woman too,
An expert in fine china,
A lover of Grand Cru.

Looks-wise, she's a humdinger,
With smiles that make men glow;
In good light a dead ringer
For Marilyn Monroe.

Her daddy has got billions,
And so, it seems, has she,
Considering the zillions
She lavishes on me.

My outfits are from Paris,
My overcoat is mink,
One hat's a tweed by Harris,
The other's silk, and pink.

My dog bowl's by Versace,
My collar's trimmed with gold,
My life is sheer *vivace*,
And I'm barely two years old.

I'm known in *the* best night spots –
A habit that I feed.
I'm on and off the right yachts
On my platinum-plated lead.

Tucked under madam's armpit,
Past cameras and paps,
I tread the old red carpet
With Clooney and the chaps.

By way of home expansion
To the basket I've outgrown,
She's built a doggy mansion,
Exactly like her own.

It's got a tiny staircase,
Designed for quadrupeds,
And chandeliers and clothes space,
And Chewy Vuitton beds.

With top-class air conditioning,
And drapes from Istanbul,
It's ideal positioning
Beside the swimming pool.

All's perfect till it hits you
That life is far from fair.
She's gone and bought a Shih-tzu,
So now I have to share.

A Dog He Would A-Wooing Go

As dogs go, I'm a gentleman;
I treat the ladies well.
A largely sentimental man,
I always ring their bell.

I'm not as half as randy as
Some Springers that I know,
Like next door's Ozymandias,
Who's always on the go.

He thinks he's in *The Great Escape* –
The Steve McQueen of Springers;
He's often getting in a scrape,
Like all true canine swingers.

The *on dit* in West Wittering
Among dogs in the loop
Is his sex life is quite glittering:
He's rarely in the coop.

The slightest opportunity,
He's off for rumpy-pumpy;
He acts with brash impunity –
He's permanently humpy.

Mind you, I blame his owner;
Jeff's one of nature's fools.
He's off now in Pamplona,
Being trampled on by bulls.

Last summer Ozzy came to stay
When Jeff was out in Spain.
I thought, but didn't like to say,
Well, this'll be a pain ...

He never put a front paw wrong
The whole time he was here,
And never caused a ding-dong,
Or tried to disappear.

We took him down to Somerset
To weekend with a chum –
The owner of a pint-sized pet
Whose name was Sugar Plum.

This Papillon, to her surprise,
Was at that time on heat;
Full marks, then, for the enterprise
Of local vet called Pete.

A quick jab in the derrière
Meant she was safe and sound,
And risked no sudden disrepair
From any passing hound.

Now I'm not one to be outdone
If offered half a chance
To try it on with anyone
Who asks me to the dance.

But when a girl protests to you,
'I'm sitting this one out,'
The best thing that a chap can do
Is take a walkabout.

But some dogs have no savoir-faire;
They'll always chance their arm.
They wouldn't think; they wouldn't care;
They've never heard of charm.

Our friends came out to say hello,
And, wiggling her bum,
Like some white doggy furbelow,
Was little Sugar Plum.

Next thing, a sight to make one quail –
A really weird depiction:
Two heads, six legs, a bouncing tail –
A beast from science fiction.

No prize for guessing what it was,
Or who was under who.
Beware the sex-mad dog, because
You don't know what he'll do.

Club Man

I'm what you'd call a club man;
I live off Piccadilly.
My dad was more a pub man,
Well known as Pale Ale Billy.

He was a huge attraction
Down at the Eel and Cockles –
A great weekend distraction
For countless crowds of grockles.

He'd stand there on his hind legs
Behind the public bar
Among the pumps and beer kegs
And crack into a jar.

But, sad to tell, drink took its toll;
Bill's life was diabolic.
He fell into a deep, dark hole –
A serious alcoholic.

He never lived to see his son
Achieve his great ambitions
To know a world of wealth and fun
In privileged positions.

But life is often hit and miss:
To cut a story short,
I moved to the metropolis,
And luckily was bought

By Malcolm, a true connoisseur,
A poet of repute,
An art collector, restaurateur,
And business man to boot.

The nicest kind of millionaire
(The nicest I have known),
He had a club in Berkeley Square.
The style was all his own:

Fine furniture, delicious food
To please the gastronome;
A calm and reassuring mood –
The perfect home from home.

And none was more relaxed than me;
I'd sit there in the hall.
I liked to keep a weather eye
On members one and all.

For owners who were well behaved
Their dogs were always welcome –
Though in my case all rules were waived,
As right-hand man to Malcolm.

I'd wander through the Whistler Bar,
And settle here and there,
Enjoy the taste of caviar,
And watch *chemin-de-fer.*

The club was my old stamping ground
For many, many years –
A thoroughly contented hound,
A star among my peers.

But then, like Lucifer, one day
I had a mighty fall.
This carefree boulevardier
Found an Afghan in the hall:

An ocean-going bossy boots;
A stuck-up bitch called Jess –
The kind that doesn't give two hoots:
My life was in a mess.

When women throw their weight about
In any smart gents' club,
The answer is to say, 'I'm out,'
And head off to the pub.

Which is why these days you'll find me
Propping up the public bar
In the Cockles, and behind me,
The ghost of dear Papa.

Dumb Friend

Old Einstein was a brainbox
Who well deserved his fame;
So how come Tom and Thane Cox
Gave their Newfoundland his name?

He can be very plucky,
With all that courage brings,
But when he's feeling yucky,
He does the weirdest things.

He licks the Wilton carpet
In all the oddest places,
And sometimes tries his armpit,
And once ate someone's braces.

He stands for ages staring
At a small hole near the door,
In case a mouse comes haring
Across the kitchen floor.

It never has, and never will;
We've told him he should chill it:
A builder made it with a drill
And then forgot to fill it.

He is a total idiot –
In human terms, a prat.
Not even T. S. Eliot
Had such a stupid cat.

There's no hint of intelligence,
As far as one can tell,
But plenty of intransigence –
Dim wittedness as well.

He'll hump an old sports jacket
If it's hanging on a chair,
And make a frightful racket,
Though there's no one anywhere.

Or eat a massive bowlful
Of biscuits and tinned meat,
Then stand there looking soulful,
Still gagging for a treat.

But is his brain so foggy?
Is that the way dogs tick?
Is he bog-standard doggy,
And I'm the one who's thick?

Labradoodle Dandy

I'm a lovely Labradoodle;
A Labradoodle do or die;
A perfect mixture of two handsome breeds –
A thoroughly regular guy.

I've got an owner who's a noodle –
An utter nitwit through and through.
Mr Noodle came to town,
A would-be Casanova;
He drives a Maserati and
The damned fool calls me Rover.

Walkies

My owner is a busy bee –
A big cheese in the City.
He doesn't have much time for me,
Or girlfriends, more's the pity.
He takes me out at crack of dawn
So I can have a widdle
And make light patches on the lawn:
His motives are a riddle.

He's not a cruel man per se,
Of that there is no doubting.
A walker turns up every day
And takes me on an outing.
And, yet, to own a lively mutt
And *never* take it walkies,
You have to be some kind of nut –
As soft as pastel chalk is.

I must admit, I'm quite a lad,
And lots of fun, to boot.

I sometimes go completely mad;
I can be quite a hoot.
I roll in every nasty smell
With Mac, my pal the Scottie;
And rush around and bark like hell,
Which drives the walker potty.

She's really quite a friendly soul;
Her name's Ekaterina.
She does a good job on the whole,
But could be a lot keener.
She's always on the telephone
In fluent Lithuanian;
She might as well be on her own,
Like Fritz, the Pomeranian.

She natters on for hours and hours
And wanders up and down,
And picks at various wild flowers,
And always wears a frown.

I'm not a dog that makes demands
Like others that I know,
Who turn deaf ears to all commands
Just when it's time to go.
And Spartacus, the Kerry Blue,
Goes stalking some poor squirrel;
And Claud, the little Cockerpoo,
A Labrador called Cyril,

And Zebedee, the Afghan hound,
All wander here and there,
And generally muck around
And, frankly, couldn't care.

It's water off a duck to me;
I never say a word,
Or ever seem to disagree,
Or give the swine the bird.

But yesterday I'd had enough
Of being messed about.
The time had come to play it tough,
And demonstrate some clout.

I'm really hacked at being bumped
By Albrecht, the Alsatian;
And even more at being humped
By Bert, the fat Dalmatian.

So when Miss Lithuania
Got busy on the blower
With motley miscellanea,
I slid off like a boa,
And legged it past the Serpentine,
Through flora and through fauna,
While gently humming 'Auld Lang Syne',
And crossed near Hyde Park Corner.

I could have gone straight home from there,
And put her mind at rest,
But, come along now, fair is fair:
Would *you* care if she's stressed?

I really don't get out that much,
I have no chance to roam;
I'm stuck for ever in the hutch,
So why should I go home?

I strolled around Belgravia,
A carefree little chap,
And met a pup called Xavier,
And had a little yap.

I had some lunch at half past two
Just down the road from Tesco –
A rather nasty Danish blue
(I gladly let the rest go).

I had a snooze, then met a bloke
Who tickled my left ear,
And gave me half a can of Coke,
And quite a lot of beer.

I thought, I really love the smell
Of freedom and release.
So what if I don't eat so well?
You can't beat inner peace.

So now I'm what they call a stray –
A freelance, if you like.
This dog can walk alone all day;
The rest can take a hike.

Gobbledogook

In dog terms, I'm not intellectual;
My word count is tragically low.
My cognitive power's ineffectual;
I'm as likely to 'wait' as to 'go'.

I can understand 'sit', 'have a widdle',
'Good boy', 'in your basket', 'get down',
But most words are an out-and-out riddle.
Can you wonder I act like a clown?

At the mention of squirrels or rabbits,
I am off as if shot from a gun.
You can tell I'm a creature of habits –
As a mate I am second to none.

I know when my owner is happy,
And it's only too clear when he's cross.
On the whole I'm a happy young chappie,
And I know all too well who's the boss.

But his habit of nattering floors me;
All I hear is a jumble of sounds.
I can't say it totally bores me,
But it practically always dumbfounds.

Is he trying to warn me of danger?
Feeling doleful about his ex-wife?
Has he spotted an odd-looking stranger?
Is he pondering the meaning of life?

Is he quoting from something on telly?
Or a poem he's learnt off by heart
By Larkin or Percy Bysshe Shelley?
Or *bons mots* by some pundit on art?

And what about all that charade stuff?
An impression perhaps? But of who?
As games go, it's seriously hard stuff;
If only he'd give me a clue.

They say that all dogs and their owners
Can communicate perfectly well.
I hate to be one of life's Jonahs,
But communicate? Can they hell!

First Dogs

We are the President's dogs. Hello.
My name is Sunny. His is Bo.
I think that's all you need to know.
So . . .
Nice to meet you. Cheerio.

Peke Condition

A lion loved a marmoset, or so the legend goes,
But found that he was much too big and suffered bitter
    woes.
He went to see the Buddha who said, 'Here's a nice
    surprise,'
And waved his hand and, magically, transformed the
    lion's size.

The pair then got together and before you could say
    'Please',
They had a fluffy offspring and they named him
    Pekingese.
The courage of a lion and the cunning of a monkey,
Together made a fearsome beast – a bruiser, if not
    hunky.

The emperors of China carried small ones in their
    sleeves,
And fed them curlew livers, breasts of quail and fresh
    goat's cheese.
The Empress Dowager Cixi (pronounced Tzu-hsi, as
    you know)
Compiled a list of qualities that Pekingese should
    show:

Among them bandy forelegs, tufted feet and coal black
　　face,
Ears like war junks, eyes like saucers, silent footfall,
　　knows its place.
In its manner entertaining, yet pure-driven like the
　　snows,
And, if faced with foreign devils, trained to bite them
　　on the nose . . .

As witness statements go, this doesn't quite describe
　　the incident;
You could say it was just another rather silly accident.
There's no good reason why Ping-pong attacked the
　　Scotsman thus,
As we were standing innocently, waiting for a bus.

To shove your face in any dog's is asking for a nip,
And for some unknown reason this chap gave poor
Ping the pip.
It could have been his tone of voice, his patronising
air,
His silly face, his aftershave, his rather nasty hair.
Or was there something more to it? Was history on
Ping's side?
Did Buddha whisper in his ear? Some supernatural
guide?
The legends of the Orient are cloaked in age-old fog –
The Chinese are a mystery. So is the Lion Dog.

Pillow Talk

A Pinscher's not the ideal dog to have with you in bed;
Of all companions he's not what you'd call a sleepyhead.
He fidgets and he mumbles, he has bad breath and he
    snores;
Of all the men I've slept with, he would top my list of
    bores.
And that includes my husband, who in bed terms is a hog.
All things considered, I would really rather have the dog.

Show Dog

Like dear old Noel Coward, I've a talent to amuse,
And I'm very glad to say that it's a talent I can use.

My acting name is Johnny (though my family call me
    Buster);
I may not be a Gielgud, but it adds a certain lustre.

Our lot have been theatricals since 1964 –
An odd career for spaniels who are straight from the
        top drawer.

My great-great-grandpa was in rep (in Frinton, since
        you ask),
As Charles the Second's lapdog in a Restoration
        masque.

He spent some downtime 'resting' for a few months
        after that,
Then did a quick voice-over for a scene in *Postman Pat.*

He broke into commercials with an advert for baked
        beans:
There is no doubt about it, I've got greasepaint in my
        genes.

He nearly landed Chunky Meat with model Patti
        Boyd,
But lost out to that bloodhound and the gloomy
        Clement Freud.

We've had our ups and downs, of course, like all good
        actors do;
My father had a triumph with Chris Biggins at the zoo.

He could have been a big screen star and won Palm
    Dog awards,
But misbehaved with Stephen Fry while filming on the
    Broads.

The family had great hopes for me; my rise was
    meteoric;
At training school my parody of Lassie was historic.

But life for dogs on stage and screen is something of a
    lottery;
My first job was in evening classes, posing for some
    pottery.

So then I changed my agent and the jobs came thick
    and fast;
I got a nice commercial for a new Elastoplast.

I did some well-paid paw work for a TV show called
    BARK! –
A so-called comedy for kids with jokes straight from
    the ark.
My agent was an imbecile – he put me up for Toto;
The fool could see I'm not a Cairn by looking at my
    photo.

Then Uggie came and swept the board with well-
     trained terrier bustle,
And you could whistle for a job if you weren't a Jack
     Russell.

I sat around and nothing came: it almost drove me
     bats;
I was seriously thinking of auditioning for *Cats*.

And now the phone's gone silent, as I dream up things
     to do,
Like writing a synopsis for a book on canine poo.

But, still, I'm very happy in the actors' home for dogs,
And my fellow guests seem happy with my wistful
     monologues.

Oh Deer

George was going to call me Clinton –
Cracking name for a dog full of zest;
But bizarrely they changed it to Hinton:
Ever since, I have felt second best.

I have never fulfilled my potential;
I am never entirely on song.
I try to appear deferential,
But how can I when he's mostly wrong?

One wonders how ever they breed 'em;
They've less brains in their heads than a swede.
I am rarely allowed real freedom;
I spend most of my time on a lead.

There's no violence at all in my make-up;
A Dalmatian's a peaceable sort;
All it takes is a half-decent wake-up,
And I'm action-packed, ready for sport.

My epiphany hit me last Sunday
While strolling in Knole Park in Kent.
What started for George as a fun day
Ended up as a hellish lament.

I am not one for making excuses,
But some smells don't half get up your nose,
And release your most primeval juices,
And thus cause you to metamorphose.

Now, some deer are unusually fragrant,
And they make no attempt to disguise
Their disdain for us dogs, which is flagrant;
You can tell by the look in their eyes.

And, frankly, I couldn't resist it;
I slipped out of my collar and went.
No dog worth his salt would have missed it
For anything, given that scent.

I could hear George's voice way behind me,
Yelling 'Hinton!' again and again.
I knew he'd be lucky to find me;
He isn't the fastest of men.

'Oh, bloody hell, Hinton!' he bellowed.
'Why the hell don't you do as you're told?'
The leaves I had noticed had yellowed,
And the landscape was turning to gold.

Though around me the summer was dying,
I felt it was springtime again,
And at times I could swear I was flying
Like Nureyev with Margot Fonteyn.

But a dog is no match for wild creatures;
As some men came and took me away,
I remembered that saying of Nietzsche's:
'Life is rarely one long holiday.'

Next morning they came to collect me
After twelve hours locked in a shed.
I was worried that George would reject me,
But he hugged me and patted my head.

I did not take his kindliness lightly –
Licked his hand as he opened the door;
And I sat in the back seat politely,
And was violently sick on the floor.

War Dog

I was just a yellow Labrador Retriever;
As a puppy, I had fun and chewed old shoes.
I was not what you might call a great achiever,
Or the sort of dog that everyone might choose.

I was not a lot more boisterous than others,
Though I didn't always heed my owner's calls,
And I think I may have worried some young mothers:
I couldn't get enough of chasing balls.

That's all I did for weeks of so-called training,
And I learnt to sit and do as I was told.
Life with Sergeant Briggs was highly entertaining,
And, as mates go, he was seriously pure gold.

It surprised me when they gave me to the Army,
Though I never really felt I was a pet,
Or the kind of dog that drives a family barmy:
Playing games all day is really not a sweat.

I still have no idea why Briggsy picked me,
Or thought I had a nose for IEDs.
I liked balls, not roadside bombs – he might have tricked
    me:
I was just a simple mutt who loved to please.

I have never had a yearn for foreign places,
And I've never been a big fan of the heat.
So, plodding round in scorching, dusty spaces
Was not my idea of the perfect treat.

Camp Bastion was not what you'd call homely;
A claustrophobic cage is not a bed.
But, with other dogs around, you're never lonely –
Though I sometimes felt a little better bred.

To tell the truth, the work was easy-peasy;
I could smell an IED from miles away.
I'd just sit there looking, frankly, pretty cheesy,
Till he threw my ball, and then I'd get to play.

There had been, they said, the odd quite hairy moment,
Though bombs smell much the same to dogs like me.
I liked my work and knew what 'yes' and 'no' meant;
I was always pretty good as a trainee.

I don't know why I got the Dickin Medal –
What is sometimes called the animal VC.
The hero's life is not for dogs to peddle –
Not even if they're fêted on TV.

For life as a search dog is not all roses;
The Taliban could often catch you out.
And no matter what a miracle your nose is,
Chances were that they might have the final shout . . .

I am one of several hundred dogs who copped it,
And tripped a wire before they got the scent,
And pushed on when they really should have hopped it,
And, like the way of all dog flesh, they went.

So now I'm just a footnote in dog history –
A name carved on a small memorial stone.
For those who know my story there's no mystery
As to who comes by each week and leaves a bone.

Canis Latinicus

Quantum costum ille canis in fenestra (*arfus, arfus*),
Ille unus cum vibrato fundo?
Quantum costum ille canis in fenestra? (*arfus, arfus*)
Ego spero ille canis vendibilis est.

Necessarium est ire ad Californiam,
Et relinquere meum inamoratum solum.
Si habet canem non erit dcsolatus,
Et canis habebit bonum domicilium.

Non volo rabbitum aut felix.
Non volo psittacum qui loquit.
Non volo crateram pisciculorum –
Impossibilis cum pisce ambulare.

Quantum costum ille canis in fenestra (*woofus, woofus*),
Ille unus cum vibrato fundo?
Quantum costum ille canis in fenestra? (*woofus, woofus*)
Ego spero ille canis vendibilis est.

Jack the Nipper

Jack Sparrow was an anxious dog –
A worrier all day and night.
His life was one huge catalogue
Of tasks to tackle, wrongs to right.

His sense of duty weighed him down,
Like Atlas pressed beneath the globe.
In village street, or park, or town,
He was a classic sociophobe.

Now Jack was never more neurotic
Than bossing friends around his home:
His attitude was plain despotic,
And showed a curious chromosome.

While other dogs, like Cerberus,
Stood sentinel-style at the door,
Jack's welcome was as generous
As Guildenstern's in Elsinore.

But once guests dared to say farewell,
Or made the slightest move to go,
From that time on, their life was hell,
For, like an arrow from the bow

Of one who'd fought at Agincourt,
He'd catch them in the entrance hall,
And there enjoy his favourite sport
Of pinning them against the wall.

Nobody was allowed to leave –
Not even those who lived with him.
They had no choice but to deceive,
Or risk the feel of tooth on limb.

To save him grief (and save them pain),
They'd sneak out through the garden gate
And head off via the nearby lane,
And leave poor Jack to sit and wait.

It worked okay, this clever ploy,
Until, depressed by winter blues,
They called a cab, said, 'Stay! Good boy!'
And set off on a worldwide cruise.

While queuing at the check-in desk,
The wife began to shake and bawl,
'It can't be true! It's too grotesque!
We've left our passports in the hall!'

They got back home just after tea;
Jack wouldn't fall for that again.
Now they were truly all at sea,
Like sad sheep guarded in their pen.

One day they gave the beast away
Following *that* episode
(The postman's better, by the way)
To Ron and Vera up the road,
Who very rarely leave the house,
Thanks largely to senility.
And now Jack's quiet as a mouse,
Freed from responsibility.

Passing Thought of a Dog Lover

Those who do not smile
At dogs who walk by on leads
Do not have real souls.

A Friend in Need

Amanda was a happy girl;
She had a carefree life.
She married in a glorious whirl;
She was the perfect wife.

Her husband, a solicitor,
Was rich as he was handsome;
A natural competitor –
A *ne plus ultra*, and some.

No matter what she drank or ate,
She still stayed slim and supple.
In jeans or evening dress, no sweat,
They made the ideal couple.

Their baby, Tom, was *sans pareil* –
They put him down for Eton.
As lifestyles go, you'd have to say,
Theirs had to be unbeaten.

They bought a little Kerry Blue,
A perky chap called Paddy.
They walked on Saturdays in Kew –
Amanda, Tom and Daddy.

And then one day her husband, Nick,
Seduced his secretary.
Just looking at him made her sick,
And life was far from merry.

She moved into a little pad –
A single girl, and mother,
With Paddy and her little lad:
No room there for another.

The day she got divorced was hell;
She sat there feeling grotty;
And as the tears began to well,
She thought, 'I'm going potty.

'I'm done with men, I'm done with sex,
Deceit and cruel rejection.
I don't miss love, my home, my ex,
But, oh, I miss affection.'

Now, Paddy never got on chairs;
He thought, 'It is bad manners
For dogs to give themselves false airs.
Why else would owners ban us?'

But as the saying goes, needs must,
As dogs know all too well.
Next thing, he lands slap on her bust –
Her heart begins to swell.

He lays his head upon her knee,
Looks up with loving eyes.
For dogs, as any fool can see,
Are very, very wise.

Scientific Experiments on Dogs

I do think 'dog psychologists' can talk a load of twaddle;
They seem to think that recognising how we think's a
      doddle.
Some say that just by looking you can tell how we are
      feeling.
That theory is, I have to say, decidedly revealing
About the human intellect – not canine powers of
      thought,
Which often can produce ideas of quite a different sort.

A German Shepherd that I know – the son of my best
      buddy –
Agreed to be the subject of a scientific study.
He simply had to sit there while these people in white
      coats
Did funny things to him and then took photos and made
      notes.
They tried to make him happy, and disgusted, and
      afraid,
With praise and nasty medicine and a furious tirade.
His ears pricked up and then went flat, he showed his
      whites of eyes;
They burst a large balloon quite near to stimulate
      surprise.

They published the results (with pics) in one of the posh
    papers,
And chronicled the details of their scientific capers.

But can one read emotion in a wrinkle on a head?
Can the angle of an ear reveal reaction to what's said?
A shepherd dog is smooth of face, its eyes are clear to see;
But have they tried a hairy Bearded Collie, just like me?

Dog Treats

I have tried every mixer and biscuit,
Tasty kibbles of turkey and rice;
And one day I thought I would risk it
With a fish-flavoured snack, which was nice.

I've enjoyed complete dry foods by Chappie,
Wellbeloved, Eukanuba and Spratt's,
But I'll tell you what makes me most happy –
That's the biscuits made specially for cats.

Arthur and Augustus

Arthur's Story:

I'm not a big dog lover, like some people that I know;
I can take take 'em, I can leave 'em – easy come and
    easy go.
So, imagine my surprise when, in the lounge, what
    should I see
But this great big hairy monster stretched out on my
    best settee.
I think he's a St Bernard: well, I ran a few quick checks –

You know the dogs I mean, with little barrels round
    their necks.
I don't know how he got there, it was not by invitation;
I guess it must have been a stroke of prestidigitation.
I thought he'd do a runner, but he lay there bold as
    brass,
So I hadn't got the heart to say, 'Oi, sunshine: off
    your arse.'
He stayed all afternoon, then after tea he gave a yawn,
Got up, went out the back and had a widdle on the
    lawn.
I let him out the front and off he toddled down the
    street –
As nice a dog as you and I could ever hope to meet.
But, blow me down, next morning he was standing at
    the door;
I let him in, he settled down and slept from ten till
    four.
He's been round every day since then and has a good
    long zizz.
He never wants to eat or drink; I don't know who he
    is.
He's one of life's great mysteries, like Santa or the Yeti.
Or why most space is black as ink. Or why I married
    Betty.
One day I may discover why on earth he's chosen me;
Meanwhile, I just accept that I have got a dog for free.

Augustus's Story:

I'm not a fussy animal, like some dogs that I know.
If someone says it's time for bed, then off to bed I go.
If I think I'm going walkies and I land up in the vet,
I never dig my heels in, or look miserable, or fret.
I turn deaf ears to fireworks and gunfights on TV –
That's not to say I like them, but they never bother me.
If people shower affection when I'm dozing in my
    basket,
I'm happy to accept it, though I'm not a dog to ask it.
In fact, one way and another, I'm an easy-going chap,
And, at twelve years old, I think that I'm entitled to a
    nap –
Which, frankly, isn't easy with small children in the
    house;
It's my bad luck my owner had to choose a younger
    spouse.

There's three of them – so far, at least – aged five, and
  three, and one,
And, speaking as an older dog, they're not enormous
  fun.
The five-year-old annoyed me when he walked off
  with my chews,
So I tasted sweet revenge by chewing up his favourite
  shoes.
The small one pulls my whiskers or my tail when I
  snore,
And the other tips my dinner in the middle of the
  floor.
I don't ask much from anyone, except a little kip,
But all I get is constant noise and pretty non-stop gyp.

I'm nothing if not cunning and I put my brain to
    work,
And I couldn't help but notice that this neighbour,
    who's a berk,
Leaves his front door open every time he goes to fill
    his bin,
So I slipped round there one morning and the next
    thing, I was in.
My owner's not too bothered, and I know it's frightful
    cheek,
But at least I get my head down four or five times
    every week.
I'd really like to live there, since the journey's quite a
    flog:
Can one claim right of asylum – as a poor, hard-done-
    by dog?

One

One has a pretty cushy life,
Comparatively free from strife,
In large-ish, comfortable digs –
You'd hardly say one lives like pigs.

One's town house has extensive grounds;
One barely hears the traffic sounds.
Wide lawns, a pond – that's all one needs;
One never needs to strap on leads
And go for 'walkies' in the park,
Or any of that urban lark.

One's owner has a Berkshire pile;
One weekends there in decent style.
One's summer hols are spent in heather,
Picknicking in dubious weather.

One loves the north, East Anglia too –
There's such a lot for one to do.
While others fish and shoot and ride,
One potters round, or stays inside.

As owners go, she's so enchanted
That every little wish is granted.
One dines on steak and chicken breast.
The gourmet chef serves up the best.

The chap who brings it in's ex-navy,
But she herself pours out the gravy.
One cannot start till she says 'Eat'.
Who cares when each meal's such a treat?
No titbits, mind, the regime's strict,
So every bowl is strictly licked.

When being fitted for a dress,
She saves us all from pain and stress,
And combs the floor for nasty pins,
And drops them into nearby bins,
And keeps small magnets in small drawers,
For fear of harming tender paws.

A long life and a merry one,
It's been a gas; a lot of fun:
A royal drama, ups and downs,
And ins and outs – send in the clowns.

A sort of canine Bess and Porgy –
Though in our case it's Bess and Corgi.

Lost in Distraction

Has anybody seen my dog?

I looked at my mobile for half a minute,
Just to check there was nothing in it.
And while I was scrolling, he got distracted.
I realise now, I should have acted . . .
Has *anyone* seen my dog?

Excuse me, have you seen my dog?

He's only a puppy. An English red setter.
You really can't miss him, he's wearing a sweater.
It's green. Like a jacket. Because of the weather.
When I say green, it's more like heather.

He can't have gone far. Has he gone to the car?
Is there really a need for this brouhaha?
But there is the road –
And that poor squashed toad . . .

Please, *somebody* find my dog!

How was your Christmas?

The Alsatian came in like a wolf on the steppes
(Rex isn't a creature who tiptoes or schleps);
With his nose on the twitch and his prey in his sight,
His lips were well licked and his teeth were pearl white.

Mrs Unthank was out in the kitchen, as per,
While her husband – a self-styled wine connoisseur –
Was dispensing champagne in the lounge to the gang,
Both determined that Christmas would go with a
      bang.

Lunch was ready to serve as the hall clock struck two,
So she fluffed up her hair, washed her hands and came
      through.
'When you're ready,' she said, and she reached for a
      drink.
'Happy Christmas! And one of the best, I would think.'

The table for twelve was more perfectly laid
Than the best TV advert that's ever been made.
The Waterford glass shone like stars on the sea,
And the candlelight danced with the lights on the tree.

The sideboard was piled with traditional fare,
And the steam from the vegetables rose in the air,

And the skin of the turkey glowed golden and moist,
And they all raised their glasses, cried 'Cheers!' and
      rejoiced ...

Or they would have done, had the old turkey been
      there,
But it seemed that the bird had flown into thin air.
They stared wildly around like our lads at Rorke's
      Drift
When the Zulus got ready to give them short shrift.

'It was there just a moment ago,' shrieked the cook.
Her eyes were on stalks and her whole body shook;
And it shook even more when in through the door
Stepped young Rex with a turkey leg clamped in his
      jaw.

The mangled cadaver lay out in the hall;
The dog looked embarrassed, but that wasn't all.
He coughed and he swallowed and started to choke:
It was clear that a bone had got stuck in his throat ...

The vet bill amounted to several thou,
And their friends and their family all marvelled at how
The two Unthanks appeared to remain so assured,
When they found they'd forgotten to have Rex
      insured.

Foreign Body

I do not like that pert Maltese;
God knows, I'm not that hard to please.

I've put up with his funny ways,
His silly homosexual phase,
His look of absolute disdain
That time I holidayed in Spain.
We've all of us had highs and lows,
And sniffed strange odours up our nose,
And done our business on the pavement,
Yet known what being very brave meant.

But some dogs are like aliens –
To be precise, Australians –
The kind that sledge in Ashes Tests,
And flex their arms and beat their chests,
And try to make themselves sound tough,
And pose as some girl's bit of rough.

And when this ratbag had a go
In Regent's Park, three weeks ago,
And came all Cantona with me
As I was stopping for a pee,
And murmured silently (as we dogs do),
'Ooh, 'allo ducky. Look at you!'

I thought, 'Now this is ultra brash:
If I can't have a quiet slash
Without some poncey, foreign prat
Delivering insulting chat,
(Forgive me if I play the ham)
I'm not the dog I think I am.
I'd give that twerpish mummy's pet
A lesson he would not forget . . .'

I didn't bite his ear, as such;
In fact, I didn't even touch
A single, pouffed-up, well-groomed hair.
But this was neither here nor there,
For all his saddo owner cared.
She swore that all my teeth were bared
And buried in her darling's flesh,
Like scorpions in Marrakech.

She swore like a Kilkenny cat,
And promised this and threatened that,
And, blow me down, went on to hector
A Royal Parks police inspector,
Who said, 'This conduct will not do.
What is the dog world coming to
When pets like little chummy here
Must live their life in hate and fear?'

So now I'm always on the lead
Because some twerpish foreign breed

Of thicko, supercilious mutt
Can't keep its stupid cake-hole shut.

I do not like you, small Maltese,
You canine Mephistopheles.

Back Seat Diver

Ulysses, soaked and muddy,
Stood panting by the car,
And Dickie, his best buddy,
Was smoking a cigar.
He reached into his pocket,
And, fumbling for the key,
Stepped forward to unlock it.
The ancient Ford Capri
Was not in good condition,
It had been in many wars,
Cursed with a bum ignition
And stained by filthy paws.
The locks were very sticky;
They'd baffle any thief.
They always baffled Dickie;
It beggared all belief.

The Merc behind could not have been
More pristine if it tried;
Such automotive pedigree
Is very hard to hide.
A trophy wife in fur and jeans
Climbed out, went round the back;
She didn't give a row of beans
For Dickie in his mac.

She opened up the nearside door
To let her Yorkie out.
She yelled, she shrieked, she screamed, she swore –
'Get out! Get out! Get out!'

The terrier was still inside,
And screaming even louder;
And next to him sat Ulysses –
No dog could have looked prouder.

Odds and Sods

I'm not a well-bred animal;
I'm made of bits and bobs.
My pedigree is minimal;
I'm not one of the nobs.

My dad's a small Chihuahua;
My mother is a Beagle –
Embarrassing for poor Mama
Who's really rather regal.

They sold me as a Cheagle,
The people in North Wales.
To do so's not illegal:
They've no need to tell tales.

They breed all kinds of mongrels
(Or hybrids, I should say),
And no one ever grumbles,
Or brings them back next day.

They give them funny, made-up names
To make them seem more real.
Like silly words in Scrabble games,
Some sound all too surreal.

My neighbours have a Cockerpoo –
Half poodle and half spaniel.
They found him somewhere north of Crewe
And christened him Nathaniel.

One can feel quite a fool, it's true,
And anyone can knock.
But better far a Cockerpoo
Than be called Poodlecock.

An Easter Tale

While walking out one April day,
I met a dog along the way –
Light brown and black, both ears well pricked,
And long pink tongue that licked and licked.

The sea below was flecked with white;
A soft wind blew; the sky was bright.
In all, a day to make one smile
At Easter on a small Greek isle.

We sat and talked, the dog and I;
He showed no fear; he wasn't shy.
So loving did he seem to be,
I felt as if he'd chosen me.

Though why, I'd not the faintest clue;
He'd come, it seemed, from out the blue –
A mutt that showed no want or need,
Whose eyes did not demand or plead.
Quite self-contained, no pampered pet,
A stray, like countless thousands, yet . . .

As if dark clouds had crossed the sun,
The day began to seem less fun.
Stray pets abroad can be sheer hell –
Like matey guests in one's hotel,
Who somehow fail to get it right
And know what time to say goodnight.

I sat; he sat; I tried to pray
In hope that he'd just go away.
Fat chance: I strode a good mile on,
But still the damned fool hadn't gone.

No collar, not a soul in view;
No place that I could take him to;
No local vet where he could stay;
No Greek-style RSPCA . . .

And then a miracle occurred,
When somewhere way below I heard
Faint sounds of laughter; high-pitched shrieks –
The sort that's often made by Greeks.

And suddenly there hove in sight
Beneath a cliff just to my right,
A little village with a square.
I walked him down and left him there.

He looked away to check a smell;
I turned and, like a young gazelle,
Up through the sun-baked street I ran,
A cowardly and haunted man.

Safe on the cliff, I stood, and there,
Alone in the deserted square,
He wandered round from side to side,
Then lifted up his head and cried.

No child lost on a shopping spree
Could howl as half as loud as he.
I came at last. 'I'm here,' I said.
He stopped and gently turned his head.

I smacked my thighs and waved an arm;
He seemed unreasonably calm.
'It's me,' I said. 'Come on! Let's go!'
Stretched out a hand and crouched down low.

His eyes were cold; his ears drooped;
His back, once straight, seemed sadly stooped.
'You had your chance,' he seemed to say,
And turned and slowly walked away.

Waste Not, Want Not

Most dogs are quite carnivorous;
They like a meaty tin.
My Wheaten is omnivorous –
He'll shovel most things in.
An ordinary Dublin street
Is food and drink to him:
Whatever lies beneath his feet,
However grey and grim –
Discarded bits of pizza crust,
Old fag ends, scraps of paper –
For Corky every walk is just
A non-stop gourmet caper.

It seemed that nothing made him ill –
A well-filled baby's nappy
Was caviar to him, until
The time he felt so crappy
He didn't want to walk, or play,
And seemed distinctly *piano* –
As dopey as he did the day
He drank a large Cinzano.

At half past six he coughed and choked,
And swallowed like a porpoise.
I really thought he might have croaked –
A most un-Roman *corpus*.
He's going to be sick, I thought,
And looked round for a bucket.
But no, too late! 'Twas all for naught.
I thought, well, frankly, Bother.
Then up it came and out it spewed –
A shapeless lump of horror,
Quite undigested and unchewed,
Dark brown with slime. Begorrah!
It couldn't be! It was! Good grief!
From some deep, dark recess –
My favourite Swiss lace handkerchief!
A miracle, no less!

A careless man who casts aside
A pearl of wondrous price,
And sees it vanish on the tide
Would dare not risk it twice.
I took the stinking fabric and
I washed it through and through,
And ironed it with a loving hand.
It looked as good as new.

That evening when I took it out –
As white as driven snow,
And frothy as a water spout
On Lake Ontario –
A waggish woman in a hat
Said, 'That looks nice and clean!'
I thought, 'You wouldn't say that
If you knew where it had been!'

Dachshund, Dachshund
Über Alles

When they sank the *Lusitania*
A year into the War,
It launched a worldwide mania
For giving Fritz what for.

They ditched the German Shepherd,
And called it an Alsatian –
Though, rather like the leopard,
It maintained its pigmentation.

But, being less exotic,
With their funny outsize feet,
It was thought quite patriotic
To kick Dachshunds in the street.

Forget the fearsome Pit Bull
And other breeds that fight;
The sausage dog is fitful
And much likelier to bite.

Well, is it any wonder?
We're really all to blame.
It only takes one blunder
To ruin a dog's name.

Dog Beneath the Skin

It isn't my fault I'm a Mastiff,
And I'm called the Incredible Hulk.
I may look like a bundle of mischief –
Not surprisingly, given my bulk.

Kev my owner's a serious hard man:
Six foot six and a football pitch wide.
You need to be tough as a yard man,
And you need a tough dog at your side.

This is where I must make a confession
That I'm not quite the chap for the job.
I'm relying on you for discretion
When I say that I feel a right knob.

Every thunderstorm turns me to jelly,
And when I hear the smallest dog bark,
I look sad and lie flat on my belly –
I'm the weediest hound in the park.

Like the Cowardly Lion in the movie
Of *The Wizard of Oz*, I pretend
To be fearless and gung-ho and groovy,
Yet at heart I'm just Dorothy's friend.

I've made chums with a neighbourhood poodle,
Who, like me, has no great urge to hack it,
And talk big and indulge in flapdoodle.
(And I don't half begrudge his pink jacket.)

As things stand, Kev has no cause to doubt me;
I'll continue to look the real thing.
Just as long as some bitch doesn't out me,
I'm as tough as a rare piece of Ming.

Up Wind

I'm not what you might call a flatulent type,
Though boiled cabbage can get me going;
And I have to admit that occasionally tripe
Will produce wind without my knowing.

But, more often than not – do you know what?
When one's owners complain of a pong,
It isn't their dogs that have put up a blot;
They're the ones who are most in the wrong.

Telly Pug

Hieronymus, a perky Pug,
Was something of a telly bug.
A thoroughly devoted pet,
His true love was the TV set.
The moment that the screen turned bright,
He'd think, 'Aha. Well, that's all right,'
And hop up on a little stool,
And sit there motionless, and drool.

He didn't care for *Downton Abbey*,
Which left him curiously crabby;
And bored with yet another bake-off,
He'd give a glance and quickly take off.
He never fancied Simon Cowell –
That voice alone would make him howl;
And frankly he would rather die
Than waste one minute on *QI*.

Most documentaries were a drag,
But nature programmes *were* his bag.
When lions leapt and zebras quailed,
His concentration never failed.

His joy was *One Man and His Dog* –
No viewer could be more agog.
Kate Humble was his heroine –
A lovely girl, a lovely grin.
On tiptoe, nose against the screen,
He'd goggle at the rural scene
With beady eyes and heavy breath,
Like Banquo's Ghost at poor Macbeth.

His great ambition was to drive
A bunch of sheep, say four or five,
No more, across a hillside, then
Enclose them in a makeshift pen.

112

The day they took the programme off
He fell into a deep, dark trough.
Most dogs would be content to sleep,
But not a pug whose joy was sheep.
So now the show was on the shelf,
He planned to have a go himself,
And re-live the bucolic thrills
Of dogs at work on sunlit hills.

The minds of mutts we cannot plumb;
Their urges are extremely rum;
So there should be no real surprise
At what may suddenly arise
When instinct more than common sense
Can seize a dog and cause offence,
As happened in the park one day,
Where nursery school kids come to play,
And throw soft balls and run about,
And let off steam and scream and shout,
And fall face down in nasty thistles,
While teachers wave and blow loud whistles.

A game of tag was in full flow
When, like an arrow from a bow,
A small black shape comes tearing up,
No larger than a spaniel pup,
And suddenly, with puffs and grunts
And lots of snuffling, confronts
The children and, with furious haste,

Has all of them securely placed
Within a sort of fairy ring,
Ruled by a would-be sheepdog king,
Masquerading as a Pug,
Eyes goggling, and rather smug.

A passer-by said, 'I'm a fan
Of country sports with dog and man;
But, frankly, after watching that,
I'd really rather use a cat.'

The Dog and Duck

You don't have to be Konrad Lorenz
To know some dogs have no common sense.
Our spaniel called Matty
Could turn really batty,
And sometimes cause massive expense.

When she felt she'd been treated too hard,
She would pick up this duck in the yard
(The duck would play dead –
It was frightfully well bred)
And present it with faint disregard.

A Springer we once had called Willow,
As if caught in a mild peccadillo,
Would take one of her litter
And carefully fit her
Most lovingly under my pillow.

A Collie we knew called Charlene
Did the weirdest thing we've ever seen:
At the first hint of thunder
She'd stagger and blunder
Straight inside the washing machine.

We had a Saluki called Jane,
Who would sing like Madonna in pain.
There wasn't much tune
To whatever she'd croon,
Though it could have been 'Lili Marlene'.

Last Post

Not a sound was heard, not a word was said,
As old Jim to the vet was transported;
From the moment they carried him out on his bed,
He was pretty damned sure he had bought it.

He hadn't been feeling too good for some while,
Or in much of a mood for long walkies.
They'd tell friends he was looking quite well, and they'd
    smile,
But he knew they were telling them porkies.

He had had a good innings with Julian and Fee
In a Kensington flat and in Norfolk,
In a smart barn conversion near Wells-next-the-Sea;
He thanked heaven they hadn't been poor folk.

He was not a great gun dog, he had to confess,
And the booms and the bangs made him quiver;
He felt far more at home and quite free of all stress
On the banks of a gentle trout river.

He had never done anything worthy of fame,
Such as rescuing swimmers and stuff,
But no one could say that old Jim wasn't brave,
Least of all when the going got tough.

And it didn't get tougher than facing one's end,
With one's owners tight-lipped in the front.
This was no way to treat a lifelong friend,
And he felt quite put out, to be blunt.

As they pulled up outside the vet's handsome front
    door,
He felt sure he detected a sniffle,
And he thought, 'As behaviour goes, this is quite poor.
Let's get on. I am tired of this piffle.'

He lay still and soft-eyed as the needle went in,
And the moment they'd dreaded soon passed.
Jim had died as he lived, a great dog without sin,
Uncomplaining and loyal to the last.

Horse and Hound

When Susie moved to Gloucestershire,
It was no serious loss to her.
Three decades' worth of city grime
Had made her realise it was time
To seek new pastures, breathe fresh air –
It really didn't matter where,
As long as there were trees and grass,
Like-minded neighbours (middle class),
Who understood the simple life,
Light years away from stress and strife.

For divorcées of twenty years,
Arcadian England holds no fears.
A handsome house, a 4 x 4,
A Scottie dog, a Labrador,
Surrounding fields, two walks a day:
Her life was one long month of May.

I say two walks, though not for Suze;
The very thought gave her the blues.
She'd never been mad keen on sport:
Why walk when you can drive? she thought.

For her there is no nicer treat
Than sitting in the driving seat,
And moving at a stately pace
Behind an energetic brace
Of healthy, happy carefree chaps
Who never show signs of collapse,
While madam sits there on the phone,
Like Cleopatra on her throne.
And, as the dogs cavort, she natters
About this, that, and other matters,
And pauses for a sip of beer
While drifting off to Borsetshire.

Now Jock, the bustling, bright-eyed Scottie,
Was well behaved and never grotty,
Except when faced with serious threats
To life and limb from other pets.
It wasn't for himself he cared
So much as for such fools as dared
To put his owner in harm's way,
And treat her to a bad-hair day –
As happened when the local hunt
Foregathered once outside the front
Of Susie's house for stirrup cups
And chaff, and chat, and 'giddy-ups';
And Susie, who was in the know,
Guessed just which way the hunt would go,
And took her dogs elsewhere, quite sure
That hounds would never find their spoor.

So you can picture her surprise
When, busy making up her eyes,
She was confronted by the sight
Of hounds and horses in full flight,
Breasting the stubbled field ahead.
What should she do? Sit still? Reverse?
She swallowed, she began to curse;
The dogs were nowhere to be seen –
Her brain had turned to plasticine.
She didn't often lose the plot,
But now she felt a real clot.

A small shape darted from the right,
Compact and low and black as night.
It rocketed towards the hunt,
Prepared, like David, to confront
Goliath and the charging horde,
And put his army to the sword.

'My God, it's Jock!' squeaked Suze at last;
She couldn't move, she stared aghast
As he tore on, his tail held high
Into the jaws of death. Goodbye?

But no. He stopped. He stood. He glowered,
Like some Leviathan empowered.
He didn't budge; he didn't flinch;
He dared them to go one more inch ...

The horses jam their hooves right in;
They're all in a most frightful spin;
The huntsmen are in disarray;
The hounds begin to whine and bay.
The hunt comes to a grinding halt;
It isn't anybody's fault –
Except that one small dog called Jock,
Had caused this most almighty shock,
For no good reason other than
The duty of a dog to man.